simple
effective
prayer

simple effective prayer

FINDING FREEDOM
and inner healing

A Model for Inner Healing

GENA AND PRESS BARNHILL

simple effective prayer

Brookstone Publishing Group
An imprint of Iron Stream Media
100 Missionary Ridge
Birmingham, AL 35242
IronStreamMedia.com

Cover design by Hannah Linder Designs

1 2 3 4 5—26 25 24 23 22 22

TABLE OF CONTENTS

The Purpose for the SEP
Inner Healing Model

The purpose of this prayer model is to show readers how to allow the Lord to heal inner emotional wounds as simply and effectively as possible. The Holy Spirit does the healing, and even the most effective and experienced prayer ministers all agree, the *Lord is doing all the work*. So, the goal is to let Him heal as easily as possible.

The second goal is to simply teach people who want to become prayer ministers how to partner with the Holy Spirit. The Inner Healing Model trains people to start blessing others quickly. Trainees complete six to eight classroom instruction hours and also observe and participate in a few practice prayer sessions under an experienced prayer minister's guidance. They can then begin practicing their new skills by using the Recipient's Prayer Guide.

The third goal is to allow people from traditional Christian backgrounds to grow comfortable praying for people. Any Christian who believes the Lord wants to heal people should be able to use this model.

INTRODUCTION

Today, many believers do not enjoy the freedom the Lord desires for them because they remain weighed down by burdens that need to be released. As prayer ministers, we partner with the Holy Spirit to set His children free, and in return, we often receive a blessing. More than ever, we all need to access the supernatural power available to us.

You will find each prayer session you participate in is different, as the Holy Spirit heals emotional wounds and restores hearts. The Lord speaks to His children in a way they will understand as long as they are willing to receive what He has to share. Each healing was unique in the Bible—the Lord did not use a specific formula. The various healings show the Lord will meet prayer recipients wherever their need.

Prayer ministers must understand God's Father heart is for the healing of *all* His children. Inner healing is a ministry of compassion. In Jesus's first sermon recorded in Luke 4:18-19, He declared the specifics of His role in carrying out His Father's plan. He read from the scroll recorded in Isaiah 61 saying:

The Spirit of the Lord is upon me,

because he has anointed me

to proclaim good news to the poor.

He has sent me to proclaim liberty to the captives

and recovering of sight to the blind,

to set at liberty those who are oppressed,

to proclaim the year of the Lord's favor.

INTRODUCTION

While journaling with the Lord, Press sensed we needed to write a manual that simply described the fundamental methods we were practicing in our healing prayer training and ministry. The Lord even gave Press the name for the manual: *Simple Effective Prayer: A Model for Inner Healing* (SEP). This manual is a compilation of the principles we learned, modified, and used in prayer ministry after training with Christian Healing Ministries (CHM),[1] Restoring the Foundations (RTF),[2] and Global Awakening.[3] We are indebted to these organizations for their pioneering work in healing prayer ministry and providing insight that helped us develop this model.

Throughout this manual, principles and prayer suggestions are offered to help guide and structure the healing process. However, they do not constitute a formula. Prayer ministers ***must always first*** acknowledge the Holy Spirit's presence in the prayer session, invite Him to have His way in leading the specifics of the session, and listen for His guidance. The Holy Spirit directs the prayer session while we, as prayer ministers, are merely facilitators.

Some inner healing prayer ministers experience the Holy Spirit's guidance as a thought or an idea that pops into their head, while others may see a vision. He may prompt you to ask the prayer recipient a question or to repeat a phrase. Ask the Lord for validation before you share a cue, and ask if you **should** share it. Sometimes the Lord tells us something, but the timing may not be right for us to pass the information on to the recipient.

Do not be discouraged if you don't understand the meaning of what you perceive or hear. Tentatively tell the recipient you believe you hear something, repeat what the Holy Spirit has revealed, and ask if it makes sense. If what you share is from the Lord, often the person knows what it means to them personally. If they do not recognize it, they can speak to the Lord about this later and ask for revelation. Be willing to risk and share what you heard, but do not state it in such a manner as to say, "The Lord definitely said," or "I know the Lord is telling you to…" It is also possible that the thought, concept, or vision is inaccurate or not from the Lord. Our humanity can sometimes misinterpret spiritual input.

That the prayer recipient feels loved and cared for during the prayer session is of utmost importance. Treat them with absolute honor and respect. Remember, you are Jesus with skin on to this person. Sessions are most effective when the recipient hears directly from the Lord, and this manual will help you facilitate the process of leading the recipient to communicate directly with Him.

As a new prayer minister, you may question a thought or vision you received, wondering if it was your own since it sounded like you. The Lord often speaks to you in a way you understand, through the sound of your voice. The more you lean into the Lord and develop an intimate relationship with Him, the more you will recognize His messages.

Randy Clark, founder of Global Awakening, reveals several ways the Lord may give a word of knowledge, especially for physical healing. You may feel something (e.g., pain) in your body, sense a strong emotion, see a mental picture of what needs healing, or think a word regarding healing. Sometimes the Holy Spirit gives you words to speak spontaneously that you had not planned to say.[4]

This manual focuses on how to facilitate inner or emotional healing.

- First, an explanation of open doors leading to oppression is described.
- A definition of forgiveness and its importance in the healing process is outlined.
- Specific target areas in the prayer session are depicted, including negative influences (for example, ancestral influences and unhealthy relationships referred to as unhealthy soul ties), false beliefs (lies and word curses), and finally, heart wounds.
- A closing prayer and suggestions for walking out their freedom follow.

The Appendices contain suggested prayers, two worksheets for prayer ministers, the Interview Form, and the Recipient's Prayer Guide. Prayer sessions typically last two to two and one-half hours.

INTRODUCTION

Our sincere hope for each person reading this manual is for you to partner with the Holy Spirit and effectively apply the principles presented so others receive healing.

Remember, what the Lord gives us is not for us alone but is meant to be passed on.

When we minister under the anointing of the Holy Spirit, we share the presence of God by imparting Him to others. If the Lord has called you to this ministry, He will prepare you. Knowing the Lord will equip you, pray confidently. Chris Gore, Director of Healing Ministries at Bethel Church, reminds us that we exert the effort, and God produces the results. Gore clarifies healing is not about our performance but rather about Jesus's performance.[5] By relying solely on Him, you take the pressure off yourself when you bring inner healing to those you encounter.

Blessings,

Gena and Press Barnhill

Disclaimer: This material was developed based on guidance from the Holy Spirit and our experience praying for others. The SEP model is also a basic approach, and prayer ministers may occasionally need to refer their prayer recipients to a more experienced prayer minister. For example, persons with complex mental health issues, such as dissociative identity disorder (DID) or satanic ritual abuse (SRA) may need more in-depth intervention.

We believe that prayer ministers need to be under a church and pastor's authority. It is also essential that prayer ministers live a life consistent with Christian principles and are willing to receive personal ministry and spiritual guidance.

CHAPTER 1

KEY CONCEPTS: OPEN DOORS AND FORGIVENESS

Open Doors

Inner healing refers to God freeing us from deep emotional wounds that cause our pain. Due to living in a fallen world, we all experience suffering, sin, and illness that need healing. Also, other people inflict hurts that cause us to be wounded, and we often hurt and injure ourselves.

Restoration through inner healing prayer is often a process that occurs over time. You may wonder how people who profess Christ as their Savior can still feel anguish. Sometimes the oppression gained access before they became Christians. Other times they may have, knowingly or unknowingly, allowed supernatural darkness or the lies of the enemy to enter their life.

Notes

Spiritual and emotional holds on a person's life come through entry points or open doors. Jake Kail, apostolic leader at Threshold Church, suggests the enemy gains access through:

1. an agreement with darkness when we embrace sin or believe the devil's lies about God or ourselves,

2. a moment of weakness when our guard is down because of a traumatic incident,

3. a legal right such as unforgiveness, involvement in the occult, and generational or ancestral sins.[6]

As you can see, Satan does not play fair, and he takes advantage of our vulnerability when we sin and are in a weakened state because of trauma. Examples of possible traumatic situations include abuse, a difficult divorce, death, combating a severe illness, or a serious accident. It is also vital to note darkness or the enemy tries to take advantage of children who do not have the defenses to guard against these attacks. When children endure a frightening experience, sense rejection, or are neglected or abandoned, they can unknowingly open the door to darkness.

Several open doors to oppression include:

- Justifying or agreeing with sin (continual, unrepented sin is problematic)
- Traumatic occurrences including being sinned against
- Choosing to believe the enemy's lies
- Contact with unholy things (e.g., pornography, horror movies, dark music)
- Unforgiveness
- Involvement in false religions, cults, and false teachings

Notes

- Any occult involvement or seeking supernatural knowledge or power through means other than God

- Curses
  - Ancestral curses (for example, abandonment, alcoholism, abuse, suicide)
  - Word curses said against us by others, or word curses said against ourselves
  - Occult curses or spells placed on us by those involved in the occult

- Soul ties
  - Unhealthy relationships that include manipulation, control, or abuse
  - Ungodly sexual relationships

The good news is all these open doors can be closed once they are identified and brought to Jesus. The prayer recipient then needs to look to the Lord and acknowledge they sinned against Him and others. When they confess their sin they need to repent, which means changing their ways. They need to forgive anyone who sinned against them or hurt them. If they had any involvement with the occult or false religions, they should renounce this involvement and sever themselves from all ties associated with the occult. If curses are identified, they need to repent for agreeing with them and renounce them too.

Remember, Jesus died on the cross and became a curse so we can receive freedom from every curse and enjoy God's blessing. If unhealthy soul ties are identified, they need to be severed. These areas are discussed in more detail in the following sections of the manual, and several sample prayers are included.

Notes

KEY CONCEPTS: OPEN DOORS AND FORGIVENESS

Questions to Ponder:

1. Do you recognize any open doors in your life or your family lineage? _____
If so, what doors did you identify?

_____

_____

_____

_____

2. What are several sins that could lead to an access point for spiritual darkness?

_____

_____

_____

_____

Notes

3. In addition to the traumatic situations on page 2, can you identify other possible traumatic events? _____ If so, list them. Explain how these could become entry points for the enemy.

_____

_____

_____

_____

_____

_____

_____

Notes

Forgiveness

Essentially, people who hold onto their hurts tie themselves to the person they hate. Unforgiveness is how bitterness sets in, and people come to believe they have a right to punish their offender. In essence, the person who won't forgive becomes a victim because they allow the offender to have power over them. Rodney Hogue, the author of *Forgiveness*, said refusing to forgive is like putting poison in a cup for the offender and drinking it yourself![7] The prayer recipient needs to understand the concept of forgiveness and its importance. (See table below):

Forgiveness is NOT:	Forgiveness is:
• forgetting what happened or erasing a memory	• releasing the *power* the memory has over you
• saying what the offender did was okay	• acknowledging the wrongdoing but choosing to let it go
• a feeling	• a choice, a decision, or an act of the will
• saying there is no debt owed	• canceling that debt
• saying reconciliation of the relationship is the next step	• necessary, but reconciliation is *not necessary*
• releasing your boundaries and saying anything goes	• recognizing it may be unsafe to be around the offenders even though you forgave them
• letting the person off the hook	• transferring the person to Jesus's hook
• dependent on the actions and choices of the offender	• dependent on your choice to forgive regardless of the offender's response
• done to benefit the offender	• done to benefit the person who was offended or hurt

Notes

A possible block or hindrance to healing can come from the person's unwillingness to forgive their offender or even forgive themselves for past mistakes. Frequently, the concept of forgiveness is misunderstood, and people feel justified in withholding forgiveness because of mistreatment by their offender. But refusing to release the anger, resentment, and pain only injures the wounded more by their refusal to forgive.

Matthew 6:14-15 declares, "For if you forgive others their trespasses, your heavenly Father will also forgive you, but if you do not forgive others their trespasses, neither will your Father forgive your trespasses."

There is biblical support for the necessity of forgiveness. Read that passage again for emphasis, for there is an eternal consequence riding on a person's willingness or refusal to forgive.

One reason a person may feel resistant to forgive comes from unfairness in what the offender did to them. R.T. Kendall, a well-known author on forgiveness, points to making a decision for inner peace, which requires a daily decision to let the offender off the hook.[8] Again, the person may not deserve forgiveness. According to God's Word, we do not deserve forgiveness either, yet God gave us abundant grace. Jesus died on the cross to set us free from the sins we committed. Was that fair?

So how do we go about forgiving our offenders?

Notes

- You agree with God by confessing your sin of unforgiveness and asking the Lord to forgive you.
- Ask the Lord for His power to forgive the offender(s). Ask Him to help you see those who hurt you as He sees them and to feel His compassion for them.
- Ask the Lord if there are any lies you believe about yourself because of the offense.
- Ask the Lord to reveal His truth regarding these lies or false beliefs.
- It is vital to recognize that unforgiveness is not an option for the believer.

The good news is God graciously forgives us through Jesus's shed blood on the cross when we confess our sins before Him. In light of this mercy, can we do any less for others?

1 John 1:9 says, "If we confess our sins, he is faithful and just to forgive us our sins and to cleanse us from all unrighteousness."

Ephesians 1:7-8 says, "In him we have redemption through his blood, the forgiveness of our trespasses, according to the riches of his grace, which he lavished upon us, in all wisdom and insight."

Remember, feelings are not the most reliable way of determining if you have forgiven a person. Remind the prayer recipient to ask the Lord continually for the power to forgive, based on an act of obedience to the command in Matthew 6:14-15. The person you pray for must understand what it means to forgive. Take time to explain what forgiveness is and what it is not before verbally asking the prayer recipient to forgive during the prayer time. If prayer

Notes

receivers are still unwilling to release their emotional wounds, ask if they would be willing to ask the Lord to help them forgive their offender.

Clarify that reconciliation does not always follow forgiveness. If it is not safe to contact the offender (e.g., the perpetrator is physically abusive), an ongoing relationship is not an option. Reconciliation also depends on the offender's willingness to resolve the underlying issues.

The offender does not need to know they were forgiven. Forgiveness benefits the offended person regardless of whether the offender knows about the decision to release, heal, and move on. It takes one person to forgive and two people to reconcile. If the offender is no longer living, forgiveness is nevertheless necessary.

An example of a simple prayer of forgiveness: (person prays the bolded words aloud):

> **Lord, You have made it clear that you want the healing and freedom for me that forgiveness brings. Therefore, I choose to forgive** (*name of person*) **for** (*what they did*) (*repeat as needed*). **I release _____ from any debt I believed was owed me. I repent for judging, and I let go of all judgments I had against _____ and any consequences or retributions I wanted for _____. I give all this over to You, Lord. I ask this in the name of Jesus.**

Scenario:

Marcia had learned to withhold forgiveness until the person who offended her demonstrated remorse or rendered fairness. She developed anxiety, tension head-

Notes

aches, and tightness in her shoulders, especially when she ruminated over losing her position on the cheerleading squad. Marcia experienced physical and emotional pain, but the coach who cut her from the team did not. Bitterness set in, and she had difficulty sleeping. Her friend suggested that Marcia use the prayer above to release herself from the coach and give him and the situation to Jesus. Marcia did pray this prayer while her friend listened, and she did experience freedom.

Forgiving Yourself:

Sometimes prayer recipients are willing to forgive others, but they may say they cannot forgive themselves. Help them to understand this inability or unwillingness to forgive themselves blocks healing because they are in the way of what God desires to do. God wants **all** of His children healed. In essence, the person who chooses not to forgive himself assumes the judge's role, which only belongs to God. Carefully explain this concept because you do not want the prayer recipient to undergo more condemnation. Remember, they already condemn themselves with their unwillingness to let themselves off the hook and release all their concerns and failures to Jesus.

Whenever we hold onto guilt, we partner with condemnation. The antidote is forgiveness. Ask the Lord for the words to speak to the person because you want to convey His compassion to them and not judgment or criticism. Prayer recipients must realize that if the God of the universe has forgiven them, they have no right to hold onto self-condemnation. Essentially, they are saying Jesus's death on the cross was not enough of a sacrifice for them. Often, they have not considered their unwillingness to forgive themselves from this perspective.

Notes

Questions to Ponder:

1. Why is it necessary for Christians to forgive?

_____

_____

_____

_____

Should you forgive someone who is not remorseful? _____ Why or why not?

_____

_____

_____

2. What are several reasons people feel justified withholding forgiveness?

_____

_____

_____

_____

Notes

3. Who benefits the most from forgiveness?

_____

_____

_____

4. Do you find it more difficult to forgive yourself for past mistakes than to forgive others? _____ Why or why not?

_____

_____

_____

_____

Notes

CHAPTER 2

THE INTERVIEW AND PRAYER PROCESS

Getting Ready for the Interview

Before meeting for prayer with the prayer recipient, read their completed Healing Prayer Ministry Interview Form. Ask the Holy Spirit for His guidance regarding areas to focus on in the prayer session. Look for their family and ancestral patterns in the responses that correlate with the issue prompting them to seek help at this time. Select the ancestral influences that appear to have the most impact on the current concern. Initially, in our prayer ministry, we selected three to four ancestral patterns. We later found it beneficial to address all the relevant generational patterns in order to remove the enemy's legal rights to impact the person. It is not unusual to break ten or more negative influences.

Notes

Identify possible unhealthy soul ties operating in the recipient's life. Select one or two false beliefs related to the current issue. You may only have time to address the most prominent lie in the prayer session. If you have time, you may address a second false belief. Review the Interview Form to see if any word curses need to be broken.

Write down the ancestral influences, soul ties, false beliefs, and word curses you identified and pray over them, asking the Holy Spirit for guidance. (See Appendix D: Worksheet for Prayer Ministers.) Also, write down any questions you have regarding what the recipient wrote and any areas needing further clarification. When you meet the person, you can ask additional questions for clarification at the beginning of the interview. Based on what you sense from the Holy Spirit and what new or clarifying information the prayer recipient shares, you may need to adjust the written, targeted areas.

One of the foundational teachings for prayer ministers who train with Christian Healing Ministries is to listen, love, and pray for the individual who has come to us for prayer.[9]

Prayer ministers first listen to the person's story and their concerns. Then they show them God's love and pray for healing under the guidance and leading of the Holy Spirit. Two prayer ministers are recommended to facilitate the session, and there can be additional intercessors. Intercessors typically do not speak in the prayer session but they can write a note to the prayer ministers if the Holy Spirit nudges them to share some information.

Preparing for this prayer ministry is essential. Randy Clark recommends living in a state of expectation and preparation because we never know when God may lead us to pray for someone.

Notes

Clark suggests we get ready before praying by:

- trying to be pure and clean for God to use.
- being in frequent prayer to increase our sensitivity to God's leading and guidance.
- asking the Holy Spirit if there is anyone in our lives who we need to forgive. If there is, then forgive from our heart immediately.
- asking the Holy Spirit to reveal any unconfessed sin in our lives. If He exposes sin, sincerely repent and ask His forgiveness.
- requesting God to give us His love for each prayer recipient.[10]

The prayer ministers should pray for protection before meeting to pray with the recipient. A sample prayer for protection is in Appendix A.

Notes

Conducting the Interview

A. WELCOME the prayer recipient. Thank them for completing the Interview Form and their courage and desire for freedom. You may want to share your excitement regarding their willingness to allow the Holy Spirit to minister during this time. If the person is not a Christian, pray for an encounter with the Lord. We can still pray and bless the person. We need to be aware if darkness is removed from the person and they have not accepted Jesus as their Lord and Savior, they may be left in a worse state as described in Matthew 12:45. Praying with them may provide an opportunity for you to lead them to the Lord.

B. OPEN IN PRAYER. In your own words, as a prayer minister, consider including *thanksgiving* to the Lord for His salvation, eternal life, healing, and protection. Indicate that we choose to *submit to the Lord* and willingly *step into the authority* Jesus gave us to take authority over darkness. Any evil needs to leave now in the name of Jesus. *Invite the Holy Spirit to be in charge* of this ministry session and indicate that we will give Him all honor, praise, and glory for what happens in the prayer session.

Notes

C. IF APPROPRIATE, ASK THE RECIPIENT THE FOLLOWING QUESTIONS:

1. Is it okay if I anoint you with oil?

2. Is it okay to put my hands on your shoulder or hold your hand while we pray?

3. Is it okay for us to pray quietly to the Lord during the prayer session while ministering to you?

For some prayer ministers, praying quietly means praying in their private prayer language. Remember, we do not want to distract the recipient or draw attention to ourselves as we pray and listen to them and the Holy Spirit. If the person says "yes" to all three questions, then move to D. If the recipient says, "no," then honor this response and continue to D. Be sure to let the person know we will continue to pray for them if they respond "no" to any or all of the questions.

D. REVIEW THE RIGHTS, COMMITMENT, AND INFORMED CONSENT and answer any questions the prayer recipient may have regarding their signed form. You will need to use the consent form designed by your prayer covering or church organization for this purpose. If your oversight group does not have a consent form, offer to help them develop one. Sample consent forms from other healing prayer groups are available online.

Notes

E. DISCUSS THE RECIPIENT'S CURRENT ISSUE.

1. Ask the recipient to describe their issue briefly in one to two minutes. If the person wanders, gently bring them back to the reason for seeking prayer.

2. In collaboration with the person, agree on a couple of sentences that describe the central issue(s) they brought to the prayer session.

F. REVIEW THE INTERVIEW FORM with the prayer recipient.

1. Begin by asking about any responses on the form you believe need further clarification. It is best to use open-ended questions whenever possible to gain more information. Use questions such as, "*Tell us about…,*" "*What was it like?*" or "*How did you feel?*" rather than closed questions answered with "*yes*" or "*no.*" Also, use the word "*why*" sparingly. Some people interpret "*why*" as an accusation, and you do not want the person to feel any additional condemnation. It is essential to understand what growing up was like for the recipient as they tell their story, and you listen.

2. Briefly discuss the ancestral influences the person checked that might contribute to their issue. Determine if the generational influences you wrote down before the interview are still the ones to focus on during the prayer session once the recipient shares their story. If new information arises, adjust the selected ancestral patterns used in prayer. When more than ten ancestral influences are identified, address all the ancestral influences before going to the next steps. If there are time constraints, schedule a second session.

Notes

3. The prayer recipient must understand the critical concepts of forgiveness and open doors before asking them to pray aloud the prayers in this manual. Briefly discuss these principles with them. Once you determine they understand these ideas, then explain the prayer process.

G. PRAYER PROCESS

1. Give the person receiving prayer a copy of the Recipient's Prayer Guide. (See Appendix G.) to use throughout the session.

2. Explain to the recipient that they will break negative ancestral influences using the Healing Prayer for Ancestral Influences after praying aloud the Submission Prayer. Then they will pray to stop unhealthy relationships, frequently referred to as soul ties. Explain what a soul tie is and why dismantling these connections is essential.

3. In the second part of the session, the recipients will break and renounce one or two lies. Clarify that together we will develop a statement of truth(s) under the Holy Spirit's guidance. If a word curse is identified, they will break and renounce this too. Explain that renouncing these areas and breaking agreements with them removes the legal rights of darkness to impact them. The Holy Spirit may lead us to address lies and word curses later in the third part of the session when the recipient meets with the Lord so He can reveal the truth to them at that time. If so, skip this for now.

4. Then we will lead the person into an encounter with the Lord so He can speak directly to them and heal their heart. He may take them to a hurtful memory, or He may talk to them or show them something.

Notes

Each divine meeting is different. It is critical for the prayer ministers and the recipients to listen and wait on the Lord. Moments of silence often occur here.

5. Briefly summarize the prayer session and answer any questions. Ask the recipient to pray aloud the "Sending Oppression Packing Prayer" in the Recipient's Prayer Guide. (See Appendix G.) Give the person the notes you wrote and suggestions for walking out their freedom. Your notes include the blessings they received when they broke negative ancestral influences, a list of the unhealthy soul ties broken, the Lord's truth that replaced a lie or word curse, and any notes regarding their encounter with the Lord when He healed their heart. Be sure the recipient is aware they may face a spiritual attack after receiving healing. The recommendations on "Walking Out Your Freedom" in the Recipient's Prayer Guide will help them resist the attack and focus on the Lord.

6. Prayer ministers need to pray to cut themselves free from any negative influences after the recipient leaves the session. (See Appendix B for a sample cleansing prayer.)

7. If possible, you can contact the recipient a few days after prayer to see how they are doing.

Notes

CHAPTER 3

NEGATIVE INFLUENCES

Ancestral Influences

We inherit blessings and gifts, such as a tendency for musical ability, creativity, and so forth from our ancestors. We sometimes refer to this inheritance as having a predisposition for specific characteristics or skills. Doctors are familiar with the impact of inheritance on physical and mental health conditions. In initial interviews with their patients, they ask what diseases run in the family and who currently has or has had these illnesses. Physicians know these conditions can affect their patients or predispose them to certain diseases. We also receive spiritual inheritances, both positive and negative, through our lineage.

We often heard prayer recipients tell us they felt drawn to certain activities, such as alcohol, gambling, sexual sin, interest in the occult or fortune tellers, and other ungodly lifestyles, but they did not know why. During prayer,

Notes

the Lord frequently revealed that this pattern was established somewhere in their bloodline. Our ancestors' sin patterns, behaviors, and attitudes, whether intentional or unintentional, can impact us today. We may not know these relatives, for many lived before our time. These generational influences do not make us sin, but they can "draw" us to particular destructive patterns. Almost all bloodlines have some damaging behaviors.

The good news is we can take authority over these negative influences, and God can heal these areas in our lives where we were wounded. Jesus gave this authority to those who believe in Him.

Luke 10:19 says, "Behold, I have given you authority to tread on serpents and scorpions, and over all the power of the enemy, and nothing shall hurt you."

Sadly, many Christians today are unaware of the power and authority they have in Jesus. Therefore, they do not take authority over negative patterns. When people acknowledge destructive patterns in their family line and then ask for forgiveness, they affirm they want the influences to stop right there with them and not impact their future generations. They are not casting blame on their ancestors but are instead choosing to receive God's blessings.

Notes

Some Common Ancestral Influences

Although the following chart is not an exhaustive list, these ancestral influences often are identified. Allow the Holy Spirit to guide you and add any other generational influences.

Abandonment	Depression/hopelessness	Perfectionism
Abuse (emotional/mental)	Failure	Pornography
Abuse (physical)	False guilt	Poverty
Abuse (sexual)	Fears	Pride
Abuse (spiritual)	Freemasonry	Rebellion
Abuse (verbal)	Gender identity issues	Rejection
Addiction	Grief	Religion (legalism)
Anger/rage	Hatred	Sexual sin/perversion
Anxiety	Idolatry/false religion	Shame
Bitterness/criticalness	Loss	Sleep issues
Bound emotions	Mental health issues	Suicidal thoughts/attempts
Chronic illness/infirmity	Neglect	Torment/confusion
Control issues	New Age involvement	Trauma
Condemnation	Occult (witchcraft)	Unbelief
Cult involvement	Oppression	Unworthiness
Death	Orphan lifestyle	Victimization
Deception/lying	Performance-oriented	Violence

Scenario:

John requested an appointment for healing prayer because he wanted freedom from shame, fear, and guilt. He said after years of rejection, he believed he did not belong anywhere. Assuming others would eventually leave him, John faced difficulty maintaining healthy relationships and continually feared getting close to others. John's father deserted the family when John was a young boy, leaving

Notes

his mother to raise three sons alone. After months of quarreling, John's wife left him. As John described his current marital separation, he became painfully aware of the feelings of abandonment experienced when his dad left home. John thought his children were probably feeling deserted by him. He wanted this pain to stop so his children would not endure the same trauma. With the Holy Spirit and prayer ministers' guidance, John broke ancestral influences of abandonment, rejection, shame, fear, and guilt and felt the freedom he desired using the bolded prayers below.

In your healing prayer session, ask the prayer recipient to pray the following submission prayer aloud after explaining the concept of forgiveness. The person reads the bolded words.

Submission Prayer

As a blessed child of God, I choose to forgive the past generations' sins and curses. I renounce all the negative influences of my ancestors and their effects on me, based on the work of Christ on the cross.

I am sorry for the ways I yielded to these negative influences and allowed them to impact my life. Lord, I ask You to forgive me and wash me clean of these sins. I choose to receive Your forgiveness.

I am crucified with Christ, and I am a new creation. Christ took upon Himself the curses and judgments due me. Thus, I break off the negative influences that have come on me because of my ancestors. I also break off negative influences placed on me by others or by my own words or actions.

Notes

Christ has delivered me from the power of darkness into His kingdom, and I now cancel the legal rights of every spirit, not of God, to oppress me.

Because I have been raised with Christ and have a place as a member of God's family, I cancel every way darkness may claim ownership of me. In the name of Jesus, I cancel all ungodly dedications or agreements made by my ancestors on their descendants, including my family and me.

Then ask the prayer recipient to complete steps 1-4 of the "Healing Prayer for Ancestral Influences" by reading aloud the bolded words for each ancestral influence identified in the interview. You may want to lead the person through the first negative influence by reading the bolded words in each of the four steps and having them repeat after you. The recipient can then complete the remaining negative influences by reading aloud the four highlighted statements for each generational pattern and filling in the blanks as the Holy Spirit leads them.

The Holy Spirit frequently identifies people they have not thought about who hurt them when the person prays. He also reveals wounds buried alive in their heart and other areas where they need healing.

Healing Prayer for Ancestral Influences

1. I confess the sins of my ancestors, my parents, and my sins associated with *(the negative ancestral influence)*, **and I forgive each person for how these influences have hurt me** *(Under the guidance of the Holy Spirit, name the people aloud)*. **I choose to forgive _____, _____, _____, _____.**

Notes

2. Lord, I ask You to forgive me for yielding to these negative influences. I receive Your forgiveness, and I choose to forgive myself for entering into these sins.

3. I renounce these negative influences and break their power over my life, my family, and all future family in Jesus's holy name.

4. I receive God's blessings and replace *(the negative ancestral influence)* **with** _____, _____,_____ *(Ask the Holy Spirit what He wants to fill you with to replace what was renounced).*

5. OPTIONAL: Also, if the negative influence is occult involvement, New Age involvement, Freemasonry, or any other form of witchcraft, ask the recipient to repeat the following:

> **I completely sever all contact with the occult, and I break the power of** *(Name the specific form(s) of the occult here.)* **over my life and the lives of my current family and future generations, based on the finished work of Christ on the cross.**

If Freemasonry has been in the family line, consider using the Freemasonry Release prayer link in Appendix C if time allows or in a future session.

Record the blessings the prayer recipient stated in step 4. Give these blessings to them at the end of the prayer time to pray during the following weeks.

Notes

Questions to Ponder:

1. Do you recognize any negative ancestral influences in your family lineage? _____
If so, are you willing to pray the prayers above and break their power over your life and future family?

_____

_____

_____

_____

_____

2. Have you ever felt pushed into doing activities that you knew were unhealthy or wrong—yet, you still felt drawn to them? _____. If so, could this behavior be indicative of a negative ancestral influence?

_____

_____

_____

_____

Notes

Unhealthy Relationships (Soul Ties)

God created us for a relationship with Him and with each other. He wanted close, Godly bonds or healthy soul ties among His people. Bill and Sue Banks, authors of *Breaking Unhealthy Soul-Ties*, describe a soul tie as a relationship in which two souls are joined or knitted together as one.[11] This creates a spiritual connection. God ordained marriage as a covenant agreement between two people of the opposite sex to bond and join together. A healthy soul tie is formed with God at the center of the marriage union. Sometimes our relationships with other people can become unhealthy, thereby opening the door for darkness to enter our lives and place us in bondage and turmoil.

Soul ties are formed when we are in a close relationship with someone, such as a family member or a close friend. Dependency is one of the critical invitations to soul ties. Over-dependence on another person may signal an unhealthy connection is operating. Soul ties also develop when we are in a sexual relationship. We are God's holy temple (See 1 Corinthians 3:16.) and should not be defiled by ungodly sexual relationships. Soul ties also develop when someone is controlling and manipulating us. Attempting to control another person is often motivated by fear, such as a fear of rejection. Abandonment suffered early in life can be the root of fear. It is crucial to note unhealthy soul ties typically develop slowly over time and can be subtle.[12]

Scenario:

The following illustrates an example of an unhealthy soul tie based on manipulation and control between a mother and daughter:

Notes

Mary, an elderly mother, has enough money to live independently in a lovely retirement community, and she is in good health. Accustomed to manipulating others to get what she wants, she tries to convince her adult daughter, Sandy, that she must live with her instead of moving to a retirement community. Sandy has a full-time job, and she and her husband are raising three daughters. Despite being active in her community and church, Sandy makes time to visit her mother regularly, phone often, and check on her. Lately, Mary's demands have become intolerable, and Sandy can never seem to do enough to satisfy her mother's desires. Mary tells Sandy, "Remember all that I have done for you," "What will others think if you don't let me move in with you?", "After all, I may not live much longer," and "It is your responsibility to care for me." As a result, Sandy experiences guilt and condemnation, resulting from the unhealthy soul tie.

We must identify unhealthy connections so that we can cut ourselves free from them. Banks and Banks believe that soul ties involving sexual contact and those rooted in the occult are usually the strongest and most challenging to break.[13] Furthermore, they report some side-effects of unhealthy soul ties can include the following:

- forfeiting individuality and self-confidence
- forfeiting a sound mind when making decisions
- forfeiting peace
- forfeiting the capacity to love others

Notes

- forfeiting spiritual liberation and personal freedom
- forfeiting good health; susceptibility to illness
- forfeiting closeness to Father God[14]

The good news is these unhealthy soul ties can be broken. First, we must become aware of their existence, and then we can break our agreement with them. Furthermore, we can then replace the ungodly soul tie with a healthy one. The essential soul tie for Christians needs to be with Jesus Christ, for He brings restoration and peace.

As led by the Holy Spirit, ask the prayer recipient to pray the following prayer by reading the bolded words aloud and filling in the name of the person involved in the unhealthy connection:

Unhealthy Soul Tie Prayer

1. By the power of Jesus's holy name and His shed blood on the cross, I confess all unhealthy soul ties with _____.

2. I forgive _____ for their part in this unhealthy soul tie and all the ways it has affected my family and me.

3. I ask Your forgiveness Lord for any part I played in this unhealthy soul tie.

4. I give back to _____ everything I may have taken from _____, and I take back everything _____ took from me, including from my heart.

Notes

_____

_____

_____

_____

_____

_____

_____

_____

_____

_____

_____

_____

**5. I renounce and break this unhealthy soul tie with _____,
and I release myself from _____. I am free. I renounce and
cancel any darkness associated with this soul tie. I am completely restored,
and I pray _____ is completely restored.**

6. I pray blessings on _____.

Notes

Questions to Ponder:

1. Do you recognize any unhealthy soul ties in your life? _____. If so, what are your next steps?

_____

_____

_____

_____

2. What adverse side effects have you observed in relationships that have ungodly soul ties?

_____

_____

_____

_____

_____

Notes

CHAPTER 4

FALSE BELIEFS

Lies

To some degree, everyone allows false beliefs to impact how they live their lives. These beliefs are lies we have embraced about ourselves and our identity, others, and God. Often, we are not aware these thoughts are not accurate, and we accept them as truth. They include any conviction that does not line up with God's Word. Furthermore, they are developed through interactions with our family, friends, or culture. These false beliefs are formed from hurts, trauma, negative experiences, and words people say to us. They cause us to expect similar occurrences in the future. This expectation then directs our behavior, which can cause a similar circumstance that reinforces the false belief. Restoring the Foundations (RTF) Ministry describes this cycle as Experience → Belief → Expectation → Behavior. When the behavior is reinforced, the cycle continues.[15]

Notes

Scenario:

Experience – Your boss embarrasses you in front of your peers by reprimanding you and saying you never complete your assigned duties on time.

Belief – All authority figures are mean and cannot be trusted.

Expectation – All authority figures will treat me this way.

Behavior – You gossip about your boss to others and do not complete your assigned duties within the designated time while avoiding your boss.

Then the boss reprimands you again (new experience), and the cycle continues.

False beliefs or lies can become strongholds in our minds. A stronghold is a place where a belief is vigorously defended or upheld. Strongholds consume our mental and emotional energy, and open the door for darkness to enter and oppress us. John 8:44 tells us the devil is the source of all lies. His mission is to kill, steal, and destroy. (See John 10:10.)

Shame, fear, and control often work together and reinforce false beliefs about our identity. The devil does not want us to live in our true identity as sons and daughters of the Lord of the universe. Shame has us believe there is something permanently wrong with us. Fear causes us to think others will see what is wrong and won't accept us. Control has us assume we need to regulate our circumstances and the people around us, so our faults and fears will not be revealed.[16]

So, how can we stop thinking the way we always have?

Notes

Paul says in Romans 12:1-2 not to be conformed to the way the world thinks but rather to be transformed by renewing our minds. We do this by reading God's Word and daily seeking the Lord's guidance.

2 Corinthians 10:3-5 reminds us we have divine power to destroy strongholds and take every thought captive to Jesus. We need to recognize and use this supernatural power.

Therefore, we need to break agreements with false beliefs and join in accord with God's truth.

The good news in John 10:10 is Jesus came so that we may have life and have it abundantly. We request the Holy Spirit to reset the defaults or lies the person believed by changing their beliefs, attitudes, habits, and behaviors.

Steps to Dismantle the Lie:

First, identify the lie(s) from the recipient's responses on the Interview Form.

Consider requesting the person to ask the Lord aloud, **"What lies(s) have I believed?"** and **"Which lie do You want to talk with me about now?"**

When the lie has been recognized, explain you will be helping the recipient ask for forgiveness for believing this falsehood. Then they will renounce it. With the Holy Spirit's guidance, you and the recipient will develop a statement of truth regarding the lie.

Then ask the person to repeat the following bolded statements.

Prayer for Dismantling False Beliefs

1. I confess my sin of believing the lie that _____, and I forgive each of the following people for influencing me to form this false belief

Notes

(Under the guidance of the Holy Spirit, name the people aloud). **I choose to forgive** _____, _____, _____, _____, _____, _____.

2. Lord, I ask You to forgive me for accepting this false belief and living my life based on it. I receive your forgiveness, and I choose to forgive myself for believing this lie.

3. I renounce and break agreement with this false belief and any associated darkness.

> *Pause here and ask the Holy Spirit for the truth that replaces the false belief. Consider having the prayer recipient ask the Lord aloud,* **"What do You want me to believe about this situation or myself?"** *Use the information gained here to complete step 4.*

4. I choose to accept, believe, and receive Your truth Lord, which is _____.

Consider asking the person to find a Bible verse that shares this truth as homework and meditate on the verse each day for at least thirty days.

Record the truth given by the Holy Spirit to replace the false belief and include it with the blessings from ancestral influences for the person to take home at the end of the prayer session.

A false beliefs practice worksheet is provided in Appendix E for the prayer minister to use during healing prayer training.

Notes

Questions to Ponder:

1. What are some ways people come to believe lies?

_____

_____

_____

_____

_____

2. Have you accepted any lies about yourself or your relationship with the Lord?

_____

If so, what are your next steps?

_____

_____

_____

_____

_____

_____

Notes

Word Curses

False beliefs also can develop from word curses or negative pronouncements. Word curses are any negative words spoken over and received by the person, which lead them to think negatively about themselves. Others can say these words, or they can declare negative statements over themselves. Examples include: *"You will never amount to anything,"* and *"I am so dumb."*

We need to remember our words are powerful. Proverbs 18:21 warns us that "death and life are in the power of the tongue."

James warns us that out of our mouths comes blessing and cursing, and we can bless the Lord and yet curse people who are made in God's likeness. (See James 3:1-12.) We need to tame our tongues.

Proverbs 12:18 says, "There is one whose rash words are like sword thrusts, but the tongue of the wise brings healing."

Scenario:

Cindy's guidance counselor told her to forget her pipedreams about attending college because she was a poor student, just like her siblings and cousins who never graduated high school. Cindy accepted this inaccurate evaluation of her academic skills and did not perform well in school. Several years later, her pastor recognized her gift in helping others and encouraged her to apply to the local university to pursue a degree in human services. This pursuit was unthinkable given her agreement with the words her guidance counselor spoke over her. Cindy broke the declaration that she was a poor student and would never attend college, and forgave the counselor using the following prayer.

Notes

Prayer to Break Word Curses

1. **I forgive** (could be myself) _____ **for cursing me by saying,** " _____."

2. **I repent for receiving this word curse and allowing it to influence my thoughts and behavior. Lord, I ask You to forgive me, and I receive Your forgiveness.**

3. **I renounce and break all agreements with this word curse, and I cancel all resulting judgments based on Jesus's sacrifice on the cross.**

At this point, have the person pause and ask the Lord for His truth.

4. **The truth is** _____.

Notes

Questions to Ponder:

1. Has anyone made negative pronouncements over you? _____ If so, what are your next steps?

_____

_____

_____

_____

2. Have you spoken words over yourself that could be considered a word curse? _____

If so, what did you say?

_____

_____

_____

_____

What are your next steps?

_____

_____

_____

_____

Notes

CHAPTER 5

HEART WOUNDS

All people experience some hurts and wounds during their lifetime. They frequently conceal or suppress painful feelings, so their damage is not recognized or acknowledged. Emotional injuries are often acquired in childhood and can develop within the family. Some families have unspoken rules that lead to denial or burying the distress. Doris heard, "You should never air out your dirty laundry," meaning do not share what goes on within your home. Holding on to family heartaches led to secrets and the unspoken rule that it was not safe to share your feelings with anyone, especially with anyone outside the family.

Scenario:

Doris buried a painful memory suffered as a young child for over 75 years until it was brought into the light for Jesus to heal. Initially, Doris did not want to talk about the agonizing event because she said it was over, in the distant past,

Notes

and should not bother her. Although Doris thought the memory was buried, it was still eating at her. Once she poured out her emotions to Jesus, He graciously took the pain away and showed her aspects of the situation she was unaware of when it occurred. He showed her He was with her then, and He protected her. Doris enjoyed tremendous healing from this personal experience with Jesus. Then through a vision, He brought her into an encounter with Father God, who shared how much He loved her.

There are many different intensities of emotional wounding. Some may result from a one-time incident, but others may be ongoing. Recipients may not be consciously aware of how the hurt has affected their lives. Some individuals allow the injury to rule their lives. These wounds impact the whole person and affect a person's physical body, behavior, emotions, mind, and spirit. Wounding can cause people to wear masks to cover their real identity, develop defense mechanisms to protect themselves, or become shame-based, angry, bitter, or hopeless and depressed. Lies (false beliefs), unhealthy relationships, or even isolation can develop because of the damage suffered. Unhealed offenses can open the door for darkness to enter and for the person to feel oppressed. We also know that hurt people frequently hurt other people.

Explain to the prayer recipient that we will listen and wait for an encounter with the Lord at this time. There is no specific formula to follow. Ask the person to *close their eyes.* If acceptable, the lead prayer minister can hold one of the person's hands while the other prayer minister places their hands on the recipient's shoulder and prays silently. Sometimes the person experiences Jesus,

Notes

the Holy Spirit, or sometimes Father God. It is essential for the prayer minister not to talk too much and allow the person to hear directly from the Lord. We need the Lord to lead here. We will ask the person to visualize a meeting in their mind's eye. Have the recipient ask this question aloud, **"Lord, do You want to heal a memory, meet me in a special place, or meet me here?"**

The Lord may remind the recipient of a situation where the hurt that brought them to healing prayer began. They do not need to try to remember an event. The Lord is in charge here. He will bring to their mind what He wants to restore. If they perceive the Lord wants to meet them in a memory, it is essential to understand Jesus transcends time and space and can heal the past. He frequently shows that He was there and did things the person did not understand or was not aware of at that time.

If they do not sense the Lord wants to heal a specific memory, He may join them in a safe and peaceful place, either real or imagined. The Lord may meet them in the prayer room.

If the person believes the Lord wants to heal a painful memory, ask the person to say aloud, **"Lord, reveal a memory to me that You want to heal today."**

Tell the recipient to focus on the first thought, picture, or feeling that comes to their mind and not judge it. You may remind them you already prayed prayers of protection and took authority over darkness so that they will be receiving only from the Lord. All other spirits were silenced. If you sense the intrusion of a negative presence, command it to leave in the name of Jesus. Once the recipient has the memory in their mind, ask them to describe what they see, sense, or hear. They may perceive the Lord's presence as a thought, word, vision, song, feeling in their body, or a sense of warmth and

Notes

comfort. Each experience and each person is unique. Have the person describe the memory. Consider asking the following questions when the recipient can picture the memory in their mind's eye:

- How old are you?
- Where are you?
- Who is there with you?
- What is occurring?

Ask if they sense the presence of God, Jesus, or the Holy Spirit. In our experience, many people indicate one of the persons of the Trinity is there. Sometimes they do not perceive anything or are unsure. If so, you can ask them to imagine seeing themselves in a bird's eye view where they look down at themselves as a bird would see them. Sometimes, they say they cannot see Him, but they know the Lord is with them. If they see or perceive nothing, assure them that God is always with them. Be careful not to place your expectations of how to perceive the Lord on them. Safely assume one or all persons of the Trinity are present. Since we often heard Jesus was present, the following descriptions refer to Jesus. If they identify the Holy Spirit or Father God, that is whom they will address.

Then ask the recipient if they would like to tell Jesus how they are feeling. If yes, they can say, **"Jesus, I feel…."** Here, the recipient will share their upsetting emotions with Jesus, not just the situation's objective facts. If the person cannot answer readily, ask them to invite Jesus to help them understand their pain and where it is coming from. Do not tell the person how they feel even if you think you know. We want them to talk directly to the Lord.

Notes

The recipient may spontaneously tell you they sense Jesus in their memory. If they have not expressed this yet, you can ask, "Would you like to invite Jesus into the memory to heal your heart?" Once Jesus has been invited into the memory, encourage the person to soak in His presence. Do not rush this step. Keep your eyes open while the recipient is closing their eyes so you can see the Lord working as you observe their countenance.

Next, you may want to ask the recipient if they would like Jesus to take them to see Father God. They can then describe this encounter by sharing what Father God is doing and saying.

Toward the end of this meeting, you can ask the person to go back to the beginning of the memory and describe how they feel now. They will usually feel better and indicate how they felt healed. If not, you may need to remove some blocks to healing under the Holy Spirit's guidance. Some blocks could include:

- unforgiveness
- a word curse that needs to be broken
- a soul tie that needs to be broken
- a false belief that needs to be renounced and replaced with the Lord's truth
- unconfessed sin in their life

If you infer from the Holy Spirit that one or more of these blocks is inhibiting healing, you can revisit them and pray as outlined earlier in the manual for these situations. Exercise caution here and ask the Holy Spirit for the words to communicate. If a current sin not previously discussed arises, ask the person if they would like to repent and ask Jesus for forgiveness. You may

Notes

want to remind them that 1 John 1:9 says, "If we confess our sins, he is faithful and just to forgive us our sins and to cleanse us from all unrighteousness." You can also consider scheduling another prayer session at a later time.

Remember, it is critical not to impart condemnation to the prayer recipient if you do not see healing. We do not always see an immediate change because it is often a process. We want the person to look to the Lord for the answers rather than focus on the problem and issues they brought to the prayer session. Focusing on the challenges and difficulties exalts them and makes them appear larger. Focus on the Lord, who has *all* the answers.

After the recipient indicates they received some healing, the Holy Spirit may guide you to suggest they ask the Lord the following questions aloud as appropriate. Ask the person to share the responses they sense or hear:

- "Do You love me?"
- "Have You forgiven me of all my sins?"
- "Will You always be with me?"
- "When You look at me, what do You see?" or "Who am I in Your eyes?"
- "Lord, what do You like best about me?"
- "Have I believed any lies?" If so, "What is Your truth?"

If the Lord is joining them in a safe place or in the prayer room, ask the person to describe the place once they have it in their mind's eye while *their eyes remain closed.* Inquire if there is anyone with them. Sometimes they will say they see or sense Jesus, the Holy Spirit, or Father God. Sometimes they will say they are alone or with other people. On occasion, people acknowledge the Holy Spirit as wind or water. You may want to ask how they feel and what they are doing during this encounter. As in the healing of a painful memory, ask the person if

Notes

they perceive the presence of God, Jesus, or the Holy Spirit. If not, ask them to look down as if they were a bird observing themselves from a bird's-eye view. Ask them if they see or sense the presence of God, Jesus, or the Holy Spirit. Most will be able to visualize or feel a holy presence. If they see or perceive nothing, assure them that the Lord is always with them. Safely assume one or all persons of the Trinity are present.

If they are not aware of the presence of the Lord, ask if they are willing to invite Jesus, the Holy Spirit, or Father God into this place. Because God brought them to this vision and He is present, have the person ask the following questions aloud as appropriate, and to share the responses they sense or hear:

- "Do You love me?"
- "Have You forgiven me of all my sins?"
- "Will You always be with me?"
- "When You look at me, what do You see?" or "Who am I in Your eyes?"
- "Lord, what do You like best about me?"
- "Have I believed any lies?" If so, "What is Your truth?"

Expect moments of silence as the person hears from the Lord. They need to spend time enjoying His presence. We do not want to rush this healing time. Once they have enjoyed a few moments basking in the Lord's presence, you may ask if there is anything they want to ask the Lord. Wait for the response they perceive.

You can ask if they would be willing to ask Jesus to hug them. This imagined embrace can be a powerful experience. You may want to ask if they would like Jesus or the Holy Spirit to take them to see Father God. The person can then describe this meeting by sharing what Father God is doing and saying. If Jesus

Notes

has led them to God, consider having them ask if they can sit on Papa God's lap. Sitting on God's lap can be a touching moment.

Occasionally, the prayer recipient may feel blocked in hearing or sensing from the Lord. Some blocks could include:

- unforgiveness
- a word curse that needs to be broken
- a soul tie that needs to be broken
- a false belief that needs to be renounced and replaced with the Lord's truth
- unconfessed sin in their life

Again, if you sense from the Holy Spirit that one of these blocks is interfering with healing, you can revisit them and pray as outlined earlier in the manual for these situations. If a current sin not previously discussed arises, ask the person if they would like to repent and ask Jesus for forgiveness. You may want to remind them 1 John 1:9 says, "If we confess our sins, he is faithful and just to forgive us our sins and to cleanse us from all unrighteousness." If they are still blocked from hearing, seeing, or sensing the presence of the Lord, remind them God, Jesus, and the Holy Spirit are always present. They can then continue knowing they are being heard. Many times, the recipient will sense an answer to the questions. Also, they can ask the Lord questions at this point.

As mentioned earlier, it is critical not to impart condemnation to the prayer recipient if you do not see healing. We do not always see an immediate change because it is often a process. Remember, we want the person to look to the Lord for the answers rather than focusing on the problem and issues they brought to the prayer session. Focusing on the challenges and difficulties

Notes

exalts them and makes them appear larger. Focus on the Lord, who has *all* the answers. You can also consider scheduling a follow-up prayer session if needed.

Other Considerations:

As mentioned earlier, addressing one or two lies the person has believed may be done during their encounter with the Lord rather than before this time. Be led by the Holy Spirit's timing. Ask the recipient to repeat each lie or word curse and then ask the Lord to tell them His truth.

If the person receiving prayer becomes frustrated and insists they cannot hear from the Lord, ask the Holy Spirit for guidance. He may suggest you bless the person and bring the prayer session to a close. You can assure the person you will pray for them to receive revelation and blessings from the Lord. Do not try to contrive the situation by telling them what to imagine. We do not want to invite any influences, other than the Holy Spirit, into the session.

If you sense the person is allowing darkness to influence them during this time, bind those spirits in the name of Jesus. Ask the Holy Spirit if you should continue praying or bless the person and end the prayer session.

Closing Steps:

1. Ask the recipient to describe the revelations received during their meeting with the Lord. Consider asking them to share ways they feel different due to this encounter.

2. You can remind the prayer recipient this experience was a gift from the Lord, and they can go back to this place in their mind's eye any time

Notes

and commune with the Lord. Encourage the person to continue to go to the Lord with their hurts.

Record what the Lord said or did with the prayer recipient. Include this summary with the blessings from the ancestral influences section and the Lord's truth that replaced the person's false belief to take home.

Notes

Questions to Ponder:

1. How do you hear from the Lord? Is it through thoughts that pop into your mind, visions, pictures, dreams, words you spontaneously say, knowing that you know, or some other way?

_____

_____

_____

_____

_____

2. Do you recall how others said they heard from the Lord when you prayed with them? _____ If so, what did they describe?

_____

_____

_____

_____

Notes

3. Why is it essential for the prayer minister to guard against leading the heart wounds phase by attempting to evoke images for the recipient?

_____

_____

_____

_____

_____

_____

Notes

CHAPTER 6

FINAL STEPS

1. Ask the person to read aloud the "Sending Oppression Packing" prayer in their Recipient's Guide at the close of their prayer session. Tell them they can use this prayer any time the Holy Spirit leads them to pray against oppression.

2. Explain the "Walking Out Your Freedom" handout found on the last page of their Recipient's Prayer Guide. Since the enemy does not want them to enjoy the Lord's peace, they must continually rely on the Holy Spirit to keep spiritual darkness away. To continue walking in freedom, ask the recipient to consider finding Bible verses that will help them transform their mind and support the truth the Lord revealed to them today. Suggest they incorporate these passages in their daily prayers or quiet time with the Lord for a minimum of thirty days. They can also thank the Lord each day for their blessings that replaced their negative ancestral influences.

Notes

3. Give the prayer recipient the notes you took. If you schedule a follow-up prayer session, let the recipient know you will be checking with them to see if they found verses to support what the Lord showed them.

4. Close the prayer time by thanking the Lord for the healings you have seen and experienced today.

5. After the prayer recipient leaves, the prayer ministers need to pray a cleansing prayer. (See Appendix B for a suggested prayer.)

Sending Oppression Packing Prayer

Heavenly Father, I come into Your presence by the blood of Christ's sacrifice on the cross. I thank you that You love me enough to want me to be free from all dark influences. I worship You and honor You, and I ask You to send the Holy Spirit and Your angels to protect and free me.

I know the devil—like a roaring lion—wants to devour me. Please help me trust in You steadfastly, win each day's spiritual battles, and bring glory and honor to Your name.

Please forgive me for all the ways I have given the enemy an opportunity. Jesus, by the power of Your holy name, help me take back any lost territory where the enemy encroached. Heal any damage he has inflicted.

Mighty Lord, thank you for spiritual armor for the spiritual battle—the belt of truth, the breastplate of righteousness, the helmet of salvation, the feet fitted with the gospel of peace, the shield of faith, and the sword of the

Notes

Spirit, which is the Word of God. I need each tool for the battle. Thank you for the spiritual weapons of faith, truth, and righteousness that demolish strongholds. Help me keep my mind fixed on what is true, noble, right, pure, lovely, admirable, excellent, and praiseworthy.

Holy Spirit, I know my actions can open the door to the enemy. Lead me to be humble, not prideful, forgiving, not holding grudges, and content, not striving for what doesn't satisfy me. I thank you that absolutely nothing— not even the spiritual forces of evil—can separate me from the Father's love.

When the enemy goes after the core of who I am and tells me I'm a hopeless sinner, a failure, or an embarrassment to You, remind me of who You say I am: a saint, a new creation, Your beloved child.

Father God, I choose to align myself with You in every part of my life and with Your Word. I submit myself to You and take a stand against darkness and any spirits not from You. By the power of Jesus's holy name, I command all darkness that seeks to influence me to depart now. Amen.

Notes

Walking Out Your Freedom

To continue walking in freedom, find Bible verses that support the truth the Lord revealed to you in the prayer session to counteract false beliefs. These scriptures will help transform your mind. Incorporate these verses in daily prayers, or your quiet time with the Lord for a minimum of thirty days. Thank the Lord daily for the blessings you received that replaced the negative ancestral influences. It is essential to be filled continually with the Holy Spirit in order to keep the darkness away. Additional Bible verses to help you walk out your freedom include:

Putting on the full armor of God: Ephesians 6:10-18

Renewing your mind: Romans 12:2; 2 Corinthians 10:4-6; Philippians 4:8-9

Guarding your tongue: Psalm 141:3; Matthew 12:34-37

Healing your heart wounds: Psalm 23:2-3; Psalm 147:3; Luke 4:18

Resisting darkness: James 4:7

How God Sees You

You are a child of God: John 1:12

You are justified completely: Romans 5:1

You are free from condemnation: Romans 8:1

You have the mind of Christ: 1 Corinthians 2:16

You have been made righteous: 2 Corinthians 5:21

You have been blessed with every spiritual blessing: Ephesians 1:3

You are righteous and holy: Ephesians 4:24

You have been redeemed and forgiven of all your sins: Colossians 1:14

Notes

You are a dwelling place for Christ. He lives in you: Colossians 1:27

You are complete in Christ: Colossians 2:9-10

You are chosen of God, holy, and dearly loved: Colossians 3:12

You have been given a spirit of power, love, and self-control: 2 Timothy 1:7

You are a partaker of God's divine nature: 2 Peter 1:4

APPENDIX A

PRAYER FOR PROTECTION

PRAYER FOR PROTECTION

(To be used by prayer ministers before ministry)

In the name of Jesus Christ and by the power of His cross and His shed blood, we bind up the power of any darkness seeking to block our prayers. We bind the efforts of any persons working against us. We send any spirits working against us to Jesus for Him to deal with them as He will. Lord, we ask You to send Your Holy Spirit to lead our enemies to repentance and conversion. Furthermore, we bind all interaction and communication in the world of darkness. We ask for Your protection and ask You to send Your angels to help us in the battle. We invite You to guide us in our prayers and share Your Spirit's power and compassion with us. Amen.

APPENDIX B

CLEANSING PRAYER

(To be said by the prayer ministers following ministry)

Lord Jesus, thank you for sharing with us the healings and blessings we experienced today. We realize that the darkness we encounter is more than we can bear, so cleanse us of any sadness, negativity, or despair that we may have picked up. Cleanse us of any ungodly temptations and replace them with Your love, joy, and peace. Father, in Jesus's name, we ask You to remove any evil spirits that may have been able to access and oppress us. Place a blockade that will continue to keep those influences away from us. We trust You to do that. Holy Spirit, fill us anew with Your power, Your life, and Your joy. Strengthen us where we are weak and surround us with Your light. Lord Jesus, please send Your holy angels to guard and protect us, our families, and our friends from all sickness, harm, and accidents. Give us a safe trip home. We praise You now and forever, Father, Son, and Holy Spirit, and we ask these things in Jesus's holy name that He may be glorified. Amen.

APPENDIX C

MASONRY RELEASE

MASONRY RELEASE PRAYER (Also includes prayers of release from many other related occult organizations). This four-page prayer from Christian Healing Ministries is found at https://www.christianhealingmin.org/images/CHM/downloads/Masonry%20Release.pdf

WORKSHEET FOR PRAYER MINISTERS

WORKSHEET FOR PRAYER MINISTERS

Issue:

Questions (Areas needing further clarification):

Negative Ancestral Influences   Unhealthy Soul Ties

Lies/Word Curses

FALSE BELIEFS (LIES) PRACTICE WORKSHEET

FALSE BELIEFS (LIES) PRACTICE WORKSHEET

1. Statement: I am all alone.

The Lie: I'm alone.

Word received from the Lord: *God's arms are around me, and He is reaching for me and holding my hand.*

The Truth: Papa God is always with me. I am never alone, and I can count on Him.

2. Statement: I will always need to be strong to protect and defend myself.

The Lie: I am the source of my protection.

Word received from the Lord: *(received as an inner witness) a sense of peace and safety in His presence.*

The Truth: Papa God is my refuge and my strong defense. I choose to trust Him as my safe place.

3. Statement: No one will love me or care about me just for myself.

Lie: _____

Word received from the Lord: *Vision of walking on the beach and picking up shells with Jesus.*

The Truth: _____

4. Even when I try my hardest, it is never good enough.

Lie: _____

Word received from the Lord: *You are a treasured jewel.*

The Truth: _____

5. God has let me down in the past, and He may do it again.

Lie: _____

Word received from the Lord: *Psalm 23*

The Truth: _____

HEALING PRAYER MINISTRY INTERVIEW FORM

INTRODUCTION AND DESCRIPTION OF MINISTRY

The purpose of the Healing Prayer Ministry is to help connect you with God in a way that allows Him to provide healing and restoration. This ministry will not provide counseling or advice.

Please fill out all applicable sections of this Interview Form several days before your scheduled ministry. Allow 2 – 2 1/2 hours for prayer time with your prayer ministers. Please sign and date the Healing Prayer Recipient's Rights, Commitment, and Informed Consent and the last page of this Interview Form.

If you need additional ministry, prayer times may be arranged, or a referral to other sources of help is possible.

Name:_____Email:_____Occupation:_____
Address: City/State/Zip: _____
DOB: _____ Age: _____ Home Phone: _____ Cell: _____
Names and ages of your siblings: _____
Describe your relationship with your siblings: _____
Marital status: _____ Presently living with: Parents |Spouse |Alone |Other
_____

MARITAL BACKGROUND

Spouse's name:_____ Age: _____ Date of marriage: _____
Please describe your marriage at this time: _____
Is this your first marriage? Yes/ No If no, please explain: _____

CHILDREN

Name	Age	Sex	Which Marriage?	At Home/Self-Supporting/ Married/Still Alive/ Age & Cause of Death
_____	____	____	_____	_____
_____	____	____	_____	_____
_____	____	____	_____	_____
_____	____	____	_____	_____
_____	____	____	_____	_____

PARENTS' BACKGROUND

Parents' Status: Married/Separated/Divorced/Remarried? Father: _____

Mother: _____

Rate your parents' marriage: Unhappy   Average   Happy   Very Happy

If parents are/were separated/divorced, how old were you at the time of the separation/ divorce? _____

Father remarried when you were age _____ Mother remarried when you were age _____

You lived with: Father Mother Stepparent Foster Parent Other _____

Father deceased? Yes/No How old were you at the time of death? _____

Mother deceased? Yes/No How old were you at the time of death? _____

On a scale of 1–10 (10 being highest), rate your parents' love for you. Give examples.

Father: _____ _____

_____

_____

Mother: _____ _____

_____

_____

Give three words that characterize your relationship with your father.

1 _____ 2 _____

3 _____

Give three words that characterize your relationship with your mother.

1 _____ 2 _____

3 _____

PLEASE FILL IN THE BLANK

I often felt that my mother

_____

I often felt that my father

_____

SPIRITUAL HISTORY

Indicate your commitment to Jesus Christ as Lord and Savior: 1   2   3   4   5   6

                                             Detached   Committed

Please explain: _____

_____

_____

Describe your present relationship with the Lord:

_____

_____

_____

Please list all previous church denominations and affiliations: _____

_____

_____

Are you aware of anyone in your blood ancestry who was involved in non-Christian teaching or who practiced the occult (e.g., New Age, metaphysics, cults, spiritualism, psychic power, tarot cards, Satanism, witchcraft, Free Masonry, etc.)? If so, please identify:

Relationship_____

_____

Involvement_____

_____

I have been personally involved in dabbling with or practicing the occult: Ouija boards |tarot cards horoscopes |witchcraft séances |psychic power |astral travel |New Age |Other: _____

_____

To your knowledge, have you ever been socially or sexually involved with anyone who practiced witchcraft or Satanism? Yes No

Describe any significant fearful experiences with "evil."

_____

_____

_____

DESCRIPTION OF YOUR CURRENT ISSUE

1. Describe the issue you seek ministry for at this time.

_____

_____

_____

2. How is your life affected by this issue?

_____

_____

3. On a scale of 1–10, how painful is this issue right now (10 being very painful)?

_____

4. How are others you love being affected because of this issue?

_____

_____

5. When did the issue begin? Is it an ongoing issue?

_____

_____

6. Do any childhood hurts or situations seem related to the current issue? Any recent similarities with the past? Describe: _____

_____

_____

7. Do you see any ways you have contributed to making the issue worse or longer-lasting? Describe them.

_____

_____

8. Do you see any patterns in your family line related to your issue? Describe these patterns.

_____

_____

9. In the last several years, have you received counseling or psychiatric care? _____. If yes, please explain. _____

_____

_____

10. Indicate any past/present labels or unkind words spoken by others to you or about you (e.g., You're such a failure, ugly, or stupid). _____

_____

_____

NEGATIVE INFLUENCES

Please review the topics below. Write next to the topic name an 'S' if it applies to you (self) and an 'A' if it applies to ancestors, such as your parents, grandparents, great grandparents, uncles, aunts, etc.

*Also, please write an 'R' next to the topics you believe **strongly relate** to your current issue.*

Abandonment	Depression/hopelessness	Perfectionism
Abuse (emotional/mental)	Failure	Pornography
Abuse (physical)	False guilt	Poverty
Abuse (sexual)	Fears	Pride
Abuse (spiritual)	Freemasonry	Rebellion
Abuse (verbal)	Gender identity issues	Rejection
Addiction	Grief	Religion (legalism)
Anger/rage	Hatred	Sexual sin/perversion
Anxiety	Idolatry/false religion	Shame
Bitterness/criticalness	Loss	Sleep issues
Bound emotions	Mental health issues	Suicidal thoughts/attempts
Chronic illness/infirmity	Neglect	Torment/confusion
Control issues	New Age involvement	Trauma
Condemnation	Occult (witchcraft)	Unbelief
Cult involvement	Oppression	Unworthiness
Death	Orphan lifestyle	Victimization
Deception/lying	Performance-oriented	Violence

1. Indicate any labels or unkind words you've spoken to yourself (e.g., I'll never be happy, successful, married, etc.). _____

_____

_____

2. Indicate any vows/judgments you made about others (e.g., People can't be trusted; I have to protect myself from others). _____

_____

3. Are you now or have you ever been in a close/controlling relationship or a sexual relationship outside of marriage? Describe: _____

_____

4. Have there been any untimely deaths, miscarriages, or abortions in your family? _____. If yes, please explain. _____

_____

_____

_____

OTHER FAMILY PATTERNS

What are some **common negative emotions** in your family line that may or may not be in your life also?
(Example – shame, guilt, fear, rejection, etc.)

_____

_____

_____

_____

FINAL COMMENTS

Please share anything else you feel would help your prayer ministers better understand you and your current issue.

_____

_____

_____

_____

_____

_____

_____

_____

_____

_____   _____

SIGNATURE OF APPLICANT   DATE

APPENDIX G

RECIPIENT'S PRAYER GUIDE

Submission Prayer

As a blessed child of God, I choose to forgive the past generations' sins and curses. I renounce all the negative influences of my ancestors and their effects on me, based on the work of Christ on the cross.

I am sorry for the ways I yielded to these negative influences and allowed them to impact my life. Lord, I ask You to forgive me and wash me clean of these sins. I choose to receive Your forgiveness.

I am crucified with Christ, and I am a new creation. Christ took upon Himself the curses and judgments due me. Thus, I break off the negative influences that have come on me because of my ancestors. I also break off negative influences placed on me by others or by my own words or actions.

Christ has delivered me from the power of darkness into His kingdom, and I now cancel the legal rights of every spirit, not of God, to oppress me.

Because I have been raised with Christ and have a place as a member of God's family, I cancel every way darkness may claim ownership of me. In the name of Jesus, I cancel all ungodly dedications or agreements made by my ancestors on their descendants, including my family and me.

Healing Prayer for Ancestral Influences

1. I confess the sins of my ancestors, my parents, and my sins associated with *(the negative ancestral influence)*, **and I forgive each person for how these influences have hurt me** *(Under the guidance of the Holy Spirit, name the people aloud)*. **I choose to forgive** _____, _____, _____, _____.

2. Lord, I ask You to forgive me for yielding to these negative influences. I receive Your forgiveness, and I choose to forgive myself for entering into these sins.

3. I renounce these negative influences and break their power over my life, my family, and all future family in Jesus's holy name.

4. I receive God's blessings and replace *(the negative ancestral influence)* **with** _____, _____, _____ *(Ask the Holy Spirit what He wants to fill you with to replace what was renounced)*.

5. OPTIONAL: If the negative influence is occult involvement, New Age involvement, Freemasonry, or any other form of witchcraft, repeat the following:

> **I completely sever all contact with the occult, and I break the power of** *(Name the specific form(s) of the occult here)* **over my life, the lives of my current family and future generations, based on the finished work of Christ on the cross.**

Unhealthy Soul Tie Prayer

1. By the power of Jesus's holy name and His shed blood on the cross, I confess all unhealthy soul ties with _____.

2. I forgive _____ for their part in this unhealthy soul tie and all the ways it has affected my family and me.

3. I ask Your forgiveness Lord for any part I played in this unhealthy soul tie.

4. I give back to _____ everything I may have taken from _____, and I take back everything _____ took from me, including from my heart.

5. I renounce and break this unhealthy soul tie with _____, and I release myself from _____. I am free. I renounce and cancel any darkness associated with this soul tie. I am completely restored, and I pray _____ is completely restored.

6. I pray blessings on _____.

Prayer for Dismantling False Beliefs

1. I confess my sin of believing the lie that _____ **, and I forgive each of the following people for influencing me to form this false belief** *(Under the guidance of the Holy Spirit, name the people aloud)*. **I choose to forgive** _____, _____, _____, _____, _____, _____.

2. Lord, I ask You to forgive me for accepting this false belief and living my life based on it. I receive your forgiveness, and I choose to forgive myself for believing this lie.

3. I renounce and break agreement with this false belief and any associated darkness.

Pause here and ask the Holy Spirit for the truth that replaces the false belief. You may ask the Lord aloud, **"What do You want me to believe about this situation or myself?"** *Use the information gained here to complete step 4.*

4. I choose to accept, believe, and receive Your truth Lord, which is _____.

Prayer to Break Word Curses

1. I forgive (could be myself) _____ **for cursing me by saying,**
"_____."

2. I repent for receiving this word curse and allowing it to influence my thoughts and behavior. Lord, I ask You to forgive me, and I receive Your forgiveness.

3. I renounce and break all agreements with this word curse, and I cancel all resulting judgments based on Jesus's sacrifice on the cross.

At this point, have the person pause and ask the Lord for His truth.

4. The truth is _____.

Example of a Simple Prayer of Forgiveness:

Lord, You have made it clear You want the healing and freedom for me that forgiveness brings. Therefore, I choose to forgive *(name of person)* for *(what they did)* *(repeat as needed)*. I release _____ from any debt I believed was owed me. I repent for judging, and I let go of all judgments against _____ and any consequences or retributions I wanted for _____. I give all this over to You, Lord. I ask this in the name of Jesus.

Sending Oppression Packing

Heavenly Father, I come into Your presence by the blood of Christ's sacrifice on the cross. I thank you that You love me enough to want to help me be free from all dark influences. I worship You and honor You, and I ask You to send the Holy Spirit and Your angels to protect and free me.

I know the devil—like a roaring lion—wants to devour me. Please help me trust in You steadfastly, win each day's spiritual battles, and bring glory and honor to Your name. Please forgive me for all the ways I have given the enemy an opportunity. Jesus, by the power of Your holy name, help me take back any lost territory where the enemy encroached. Heal any damage he has inflicted.

Mighty Lord, thank You for spiritual armor for the spiritual battle—the belt of truth, the breastplate of righteousness, the helmet of salvation, the feet fitted with the gospel of peace, the shield of faith, and the sword of the Spirit, which is the Word of God. I need each tool for the battle. Thank you for the spiritual weapons of faith, truth, and righteousness that demolish strongholds. Help me keep my mind fixed on what is true, noble, right, pure, lovely, admirable, excellent, and praiseworthy.

Holy Spirit, I know my actions can open the door to the enemy. Lead me to be humble, not prideful, forgiving, not holding grudges, and content, not striving for what doesn't satisfy me. I thank you that absolutely nothing—not even the spiritual forces of evil—can separate me from the Father's love.

When the enemy goes after the core of who I am by telling me I'm a hopeless sinner, a failure, or an embarrassment to You, remind me of who You say I am: a saint, a new creation, Your beloved child.

Father God, I choose to align myself with You in every part of my life and with Your Word. I submit myself to You and take a stand against darkness and any spirits not from You. By the power of Jesus's holy name, I command all darkness that seeks to influence me to depart now. Amen.

Walking Out Your Freedom

To continue walking in freedom, find Bible verses that support the truth the Lord revealed to you in the prayer session to counteract false beliefs. These scriptures will help transform your mind.

Incorporate these verses in daily prayers, or your quiet time with the Lord, for a minimum of thirty days. Thank the Lord daily for the blessings you received that replaced the negative ancestral influences. It is essential to be filled continually with the Holy Spirit in order to keep the darkness away. Additional Bible verses to help you walk out your freedom include:

Putting on the full armor of God: Ephesians 6:10-18

Renewing your mind: Romans 12:2; 2 Corinthians 10:4-6; Philippians 4:8-9

Guarding your tongue: Psalm 141:3; Matthew 12:34-37

Healing your heart wounds: Psalm 23:2-3; Psalm 147:3; Luke 4:18

Resisting darkness: James 4:7

How God Sees You

You are a child of God: John 1:12

You are justified by Christ: Romans 5:1

You are free from condemnation: Romans 8:1

You have the mind of Christ: 1 Corinthians 2:16

You have been made righteous: 2 Corinthians 5:21

You have been blessed with every spiritual blessing: Ephesians 1:3

You are righteous and holy: Ephesians 4:24

You have been redeemed and forgiven of all your sins: Colossians 1:14

You are a dwelling place for Christ. He lives in you: Colossians 1:27

You are complete in Christ: Colossians 2:9-10

You are chosen of God, holy, and dearly loved: Colossians 3:12

You have been given a spirit of power, love, and self-control: 2 Timothy 1:7

You are a partaker of God's divine nature: 2 Peter 1:4

Notes

1. Website for Christian Healing Ministries; https://www.christianhealingmin.org
2. Website for Restoring the Foundations; https://www.restoringthefoundations.org
3. Website for Global Awakening; https://globalawakening.com
4. Randy Clark, *Ministry Team Training Manual* (Mechanicsburg, PA: Apostolic Network of Global Awakening, 2018), 67.
5. Chris Gore, *Walking in Supernatural Healing Power* (Shippensburg, PA: Destiny Image, 2013), 37, 43.
6. Jake Kail, *Can a Christian Have a Demon? Biblical Insights into a Controversial Question* (Columbia, SC: CreateSpace Independent Publishing Platform, 2014), 47-53.
7. Rodney Hogue, *Forgiveness* (Abilene, TX: Rodney Hogue Ministries, 2008), 27.
8. R. T. Kendall, *Revised and Updated Total Forgiveness,* (Lake Mary, FL: Charisma House, 2007), 6.
9. Francis and Judith MacNutt Training Center, *School of Healing Prayer: Level I* (Jacksonville, FL: Christian Healing Ministries, 2007), 49.
10. Paraphrased from Randy Clark, *Power to Heal: Keys to Activating God's Healing Power in Your Life* (Shippensburg, PA: Destiny Image, 2015), 84.
11. Bill Banks and Sue Banks, *Breaking Unhealthy Soul-Ties* (Kirkwood, MO: Impact Christian Books, 2011), 16.
12. Banks and Banks, *Breaking Unhealthy Soul-Ties,* 58, 62.
13. Banks and Banks, *Breaking Unhealthy Soul-Ties,* 122.
14. Banks and Banks, *Breaking Unhealthy Soul-Ties,* 113-115.
15. Restoring the Foundations, *Healing and Freedom* (Hendersonville, NC: Restoring the Foundations, 2016), 37-38.
16. Restoring the Foundations, *Healing and Freedom,* 40.

About the Authors

Gena and Press Barnhill have been married for more than forty eight years. They have two children and five grandchildren. Gena's career included positions as a registered nurse, school counselor, school psychologist, behavior analyst, and autism consultant. She concluded her professional work as a university professor in special education. Gena earned her Ph.D. in 2000 and retired from university teaching at the end of 2017.

Press had a varied career in business and received his doctorate in business in 2002. He taught for the University of Saint Mary and Liberty University for sixteen years before retirement at the end of 2017. In 2010, he began learning and practicing healing prayer, and Gena soon joined him. After completing Christian Healing Ministries' (CHM) four healing prayer training levels, they helped facilitate others' training. Later training included earning certification as Issue-focused Ministers by Restoring the Foundations (RTF).

Gena and Press have provided inner healing prayer sessions to hundreds of people, including over 200 men in a prison ministry. They also attended numerous conferences and training on healing and deliverance through Global Awakening, CHM, and RTF. Their passion is to partner with the Lord in setting His children free.

Authors' Notes

Thank you for purchasing the *SEP* manual. We pray you will find this to be a valuable resource on healing prayer and how you can partner with the Holy Spirit to heal people.

Gena Barnhill's book *Freedom from Brokenness* is an extension of the lessons learned as a healing prayer minister using our SEP model. It provides spiritual and practical insights into how Holy Spirit-led prayer can heal heart wounds and guide a person to find their true identity in Christ.

We have prayed with hundreds of people, including more than 200 men in a prison ministry. Stories and the miracles shared in healing prayer sessions are interwoven throughout her book, along with stories and lessons learned from Gena's life, to encourage and inspire others.

Press has written the "Freedom in Healing" series of novels on healing prayer and spiritual warfare. The series begins with the novella, *The Awakening*. The first full-length novel, *The Battle,* released in early 2022 and tells the story of a healing prayer team from the fictional town of Rockton, Indiana. Darleen Wilson and her six-member team pray for a former witch. This leads to spiritual battles with a local coven of witches. Darleen's team become aware of the dark spirits working against the churches in their area. The prayer team is directed through dreams and visions to take a seven-day ocean cruise to help a ship under spiritual attack.

If you have not already read the prequel, *The Awakening*, please consider ordering a copy to learn of the challenges Darleen faced to develop the prayer team.

You can get *The Awakening* from Amazon.com, our website https://simpleeffectiveprayer.com/ (free eBook) or request a copy from your favorite bookstore. If you have questions or want a signed copy of any of our books, please contact us at sepprayer@yahoo.com.

Next in the series will be *The Revenge,* and the prayer team faces increased spiritual warfare from forces seeking to avenge their failure in *The Battle.*

We ask that if you buy a copy of any of our books on Amazon.com, you would consider posting a review.

  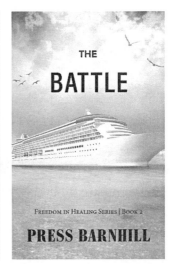